Thurber & Company

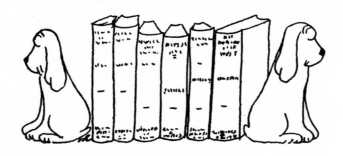

BOOKS BY JAMES THURBER

Credo and Curios
Lantern and Lances
The Years with Ross
Alarms and Diversions
The Wonderful O
Further Fables for Our Time
Thurber's Dogs
Thurber Country
The Thurber Album
The 13 Clocks
The Beast in Me and Other Animals
The White Deer
The Thurber Carnival
The Great Quillow
Men, Women and Dogs
Many Moons
My World—and Welcome to It
Fables for Our Time
The Last Flower
Let Your Mind Alone
The Middle-Aged Man on the Flying Trapeze
My Life and Hard Times
The Seal in the Bedroom
The Owl in the Attic
Is Sex Necessary? (with E. B. White)

PLAY

The Male Animal (with Elliott Nugent)

REVUE

A Thurber Carnival

Thurber & Company

Introduction by Helen Thurber

Harper & Row, Publishers: New York, Evanston, and London

Of the drawings in this book, one hundred and five first appeared in *The New Yorker*, some with slightly different captions. These include decorative spots, series and one cover of the magazine (p. 107).

The drawing on p. 1 appeared originally in *PM* (copyright 1940 by *PM*); those on pp. 11, 14, 60, 133, and 180 in *The Bermudian;* those on pp. 24 through 29 in a British magazine, *Night and Day;* those on pp. 36 through 41 in the Ohio State University *Sundial;* and those on pp. 119 through 125 in *Stage Magazine* (copyright 1935 by Stage Publishing Company, Inc.). Except for *The Patient* series, none of these drawings has ever appeared in book form, and those on pp. 4, 68, 74, 94 through 99, 128 through 132, 135 through 141, 168, 169, and 181 are from private collections and have never been published before.

Grateful acknowledgment is made to Harcourt, Brace & World, Inc., for the use of a number of drawings from *Men, Women and Dogs,* published in 1943, and from *The Beast in Me,* published in 1948.

Acknowledgment is also made for a few drawings from *Thurber's Dogs,* published by Simon and Schuster, Inc., in 1955.

THURBER & COMPANY.

FIRST EDITION

LIBRARY OF CONGRESS CATALOG CARD NUMBER: 64-18067

CONTENTS

INTRODUCTION

Since the day many months ago when I innocently began to select Thurber drawings for this collection, a number of unexpected and remarkable things have turned up. In the attic, an old roll-top desk dating back to our first New York apartment disgorged, along with a small chunk of wedding cake and our Guaranty Trust bank statements for 1935, the original sketch of my favorite Ophelia (maybe not Richard Burton's favorite Ophelia, but definitely my favorite Ophelia), and the other Shakespeare illustrations shown in this book. Thurber's interpretation of Edgar Allan Poe's *The Raven,* never seen before or long forgotten, fell out of a beaten-up file folder, and in a slim envelope with the marks of a snapped elastic band still on it, and the cryptic notation, "1917-1918," I found a few pages torn out of the Ohio State *Sundial* for those years, when one James Grover Thurber was editor.

One or two of these look to me like *art nouveau,* done in a period when art was indeed *nouveau.* Today (or, hopefully, yesterday) they could even be called Camp, but I doubt if Thurber would have used that word. Perhaps in his youth the stained-glass bay windows along the streets of Columbus, Ohio, did conceal such horrendous interiors, but I swear that some of the furniture must have existed only in the artist's imagination, already playfully at work. What, for instance, is that large urnlike object in the right background on p. 41? I wish I knew.

Just as unexpectedly, old friends dipped into their private collections and provided me with drawings never published. One of them sent me a letter and a few rough sketches commemorating the first meeting of Carl Sandburg and James Thurber at a late-evening dinner in the home of a bewildered Columbus hostess. These are, I'm afraid, only pale reflections of what really went on that night. It was, as always with Carl Sandburg, a wild and wonderful occasion.

From others I got Thurber's impressions of Paris and Rome as he saw them in 1937 and 1938. One ingenious friend even brought me an old tablecloth from Tim Costello's Third Avenue bar, used at a birthday celebration many years ago. Jim could evidently draw as he drank, for it was covered with his men and women and dogs. The cloth got badly stained with steak juice and Scotch during the long evening, but one of the female guests, famous for her needlework, took it home, embroidered the scrawls to preserve them, and had the whole thing laundered for posterity. It was a little too unwieldy for this book, but looks just dandy on the tea table.

This might be the time to hear a few comments about Thurber drawings in general. My husband never cared much for the label of cartoonist, but he was equally reluctant about being called an artist. He had so much fun drawing pictures that he never really took them seriously. E. B. White has remarked that in Thurber drawings "one finds not only the simple themes of love and misunderstanding, but also the rarer and tenderer insupportabilities." Sterner critics, usually the parents of young children, have written that their four-year-old daughter could do better, and some have even proved it by enclosing a few childish scrawls that bore the unmistakable mark (I hardly dare call it promise) of a mature Thurber.

Except for Mr. White's perception, and the witty eloquence of Dorothy Parker, who once described Thurber men and women as having "the outer semblance of unbaked cookies," perhaps the best comments on his work have been made by Thurber himself. It's one of the joys of an editor to be able to quote the author (it's also the laziest way to write an Introduction), so I shall now turn the floor over to the artist, who at one time or another has made these confessions:

"I went back over my drawings in the wistful hope that I would find evidence on which to base a fond belief that my work, or fun, had somehow improved. . . . The only change I could find, however, in comparing old and recent scrawls, was a certain tightening of my lack of technique over the eras, the inevitable and impure result of constant practice. In the case of a man who cannot draw, but keeps on drawing anyway, practice pays in meagre coin for what it takes away."

"The editors want to know if it is true that I draw by moonlight, or under water, and when I say no, they lose interest."

"My drawings sometimes seem to have reached completion by some other route than the common one of intent. They have been described as pre-intentionalist, meaning that they were finished before the ideas for them had occurred to me. I shall not argue the point."

And finally: "The State Police questioned us all, and did not come off very well with me. 'What kind of an artist are you?' a detective asked me, and I must have looked guilty as hell. I finally said, 'I refuse to answer that question on the ground that it might incriminate me.' "

Well, that should give you some idea of what to expect, if you don't know already. And now I would like to make a few acknowledgments. For their useful advice and criticism, I want to thank Roz Algrant, Haila Stoddard, and Whitfield Connor. I am grateful to Jap and Helen Gude, John and Madeline Miller, Walter Goetz, Florence Perry, Ruth Hawkins, Dorothy Miller and Ronald and Jane Williams for sharing their private collections with me; to Fritzi von Kuegelgen and Juliette Bleesz for helping me sift and select; and most of all, I give thanks for Marc Simont, artist and old friend of the Thurbers, who gave his time and talent to the creative work of putting *Thurber & Company* together.

HELEN THURBER

West Cornwall, Connecticut
April, 1966

Sports

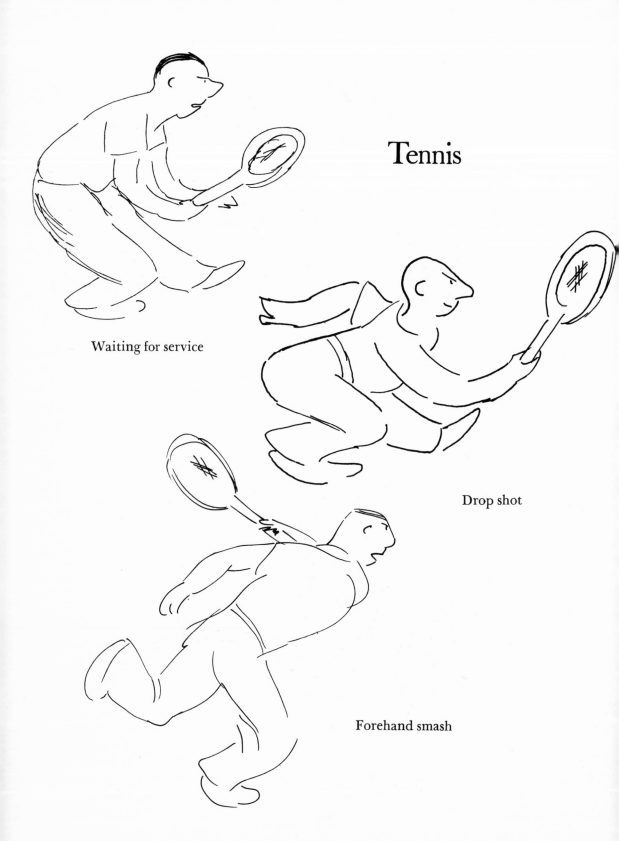

Tennis

Waiting for service

Drop shot

Forehand smash

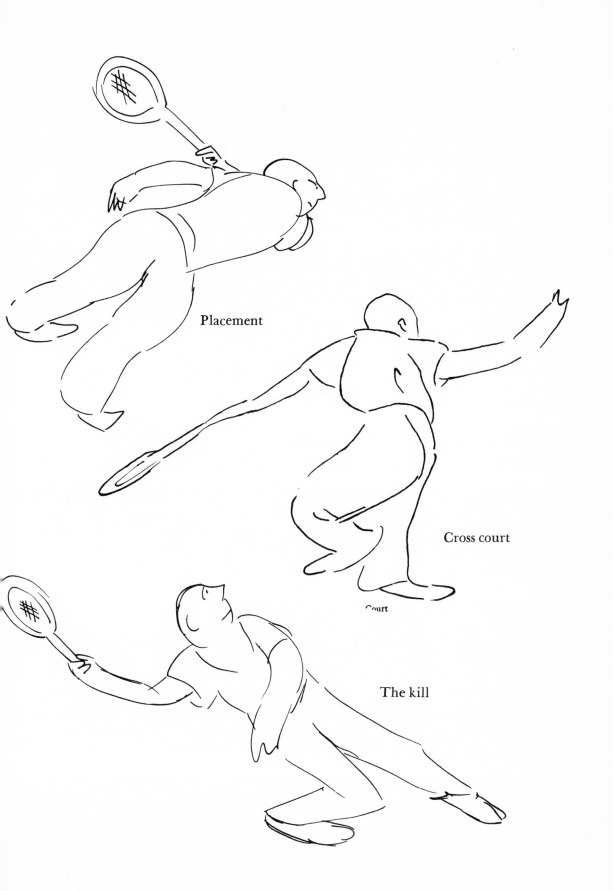

Placement

Cross court

Court

The kill

"Look out, Harry!"

"I can tell you right now that isn't going to work."

"Other end, Mr. Pemberton."

"Stop me!"

"Mamma always gets sore and spoils the game for everybody."

The Patient

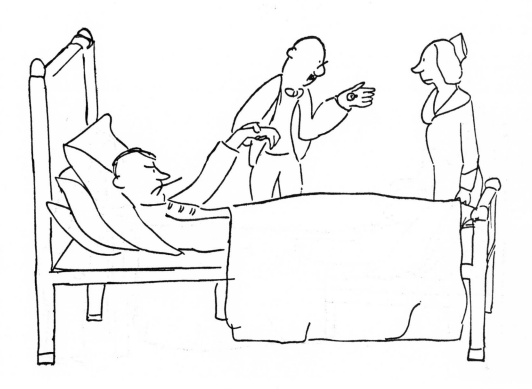

Pulse and temperature

A fit of temper

A nurse tells him the plot of "Miracle of the Bells."

Lunch time again

The doctor describes a streptococcus case.

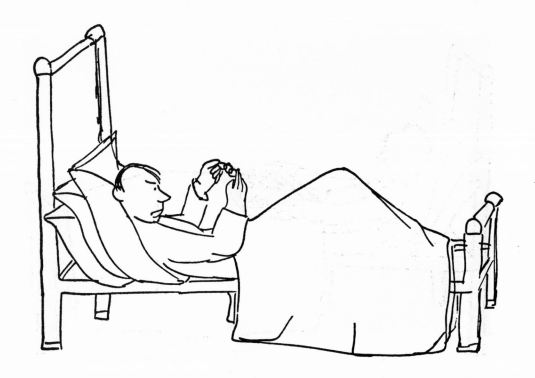

The linked puzzle

Momentary content: The sports page

Black Doubt: Is his wife out with an old beau?

The jolly visitors

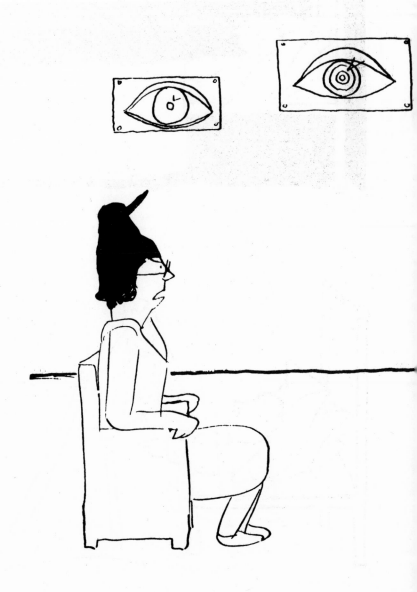

"Certainly I can make it out! It's three sea horses and an 'h'."

"Dr. Livingstone, I presume?"

"My analyst is crazy to meet you, darling."

"Your ailment is on the tip of my tongue, Mrs. Cartright—let me think."

"I can't stand to have my pulse felt, Doctor!"

"I never really rallied after the birth of my first child."

"I keep toying with the idea of suicide, Doctor."

1917-1918

Christmas near South Bend, Indiana

Christmas north of Carson City, Nevada

Christmas not far from Omaha, Nebraska

Christmas southeast of Portland, Oregon

Mainly Men and Women

1

"I'm getting tired of you throwing your weight around."

"You keep your wife's name out of this, Ashby!"

"Sometimes the news from Washington forces me to the conclusion
that your mother and your brother Ed are in charge."

"Why don't you let me know what it is, if it's so pleasant?"

"That martyred look won't get you anywhere with me."

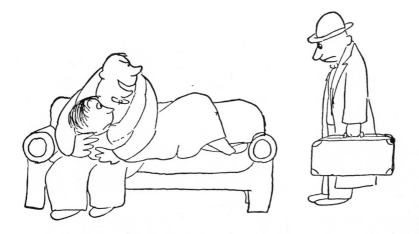

"The eternal feminine, Mr. Blake, the eternal feminine!"

"You're the only woman that ever let me alone."

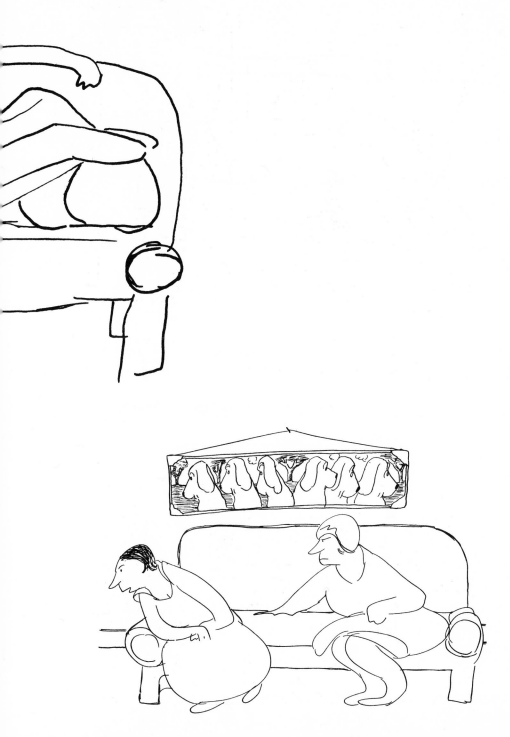

"I yielded, yes—but I never led your husband on, Mrs. Fisher."

"I don't know them, either, dear, but there may be some simple explanation."

"Maybe you don't have charm, Lily, but you're enigmatic."

"What do you want me to do with your remains, George?"

"I'm afraid you are in the wrong apartment, Madam."

"She's reading some novel that's breaking her heart,
but we don't know where she hides it."

"Why did I ever marry below my emotional level?"

Fantasies

End of Paved Road

Death Comes for the Dowager

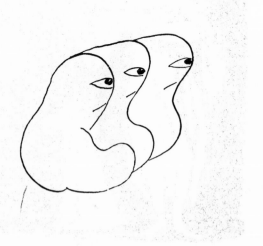

The Awakening of Spring

Scylla

Ad Astra

The Furies

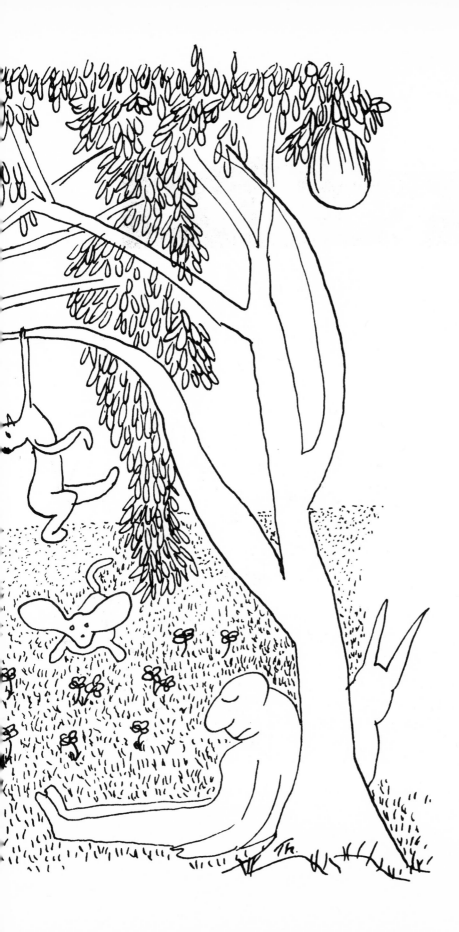

Opportunity

A Gallery of
Real Creatures

The Northern Lynx

The Lapp Owl

The Cynogale

The Awantibo

The Tarsier

The Cape-Maned Lion

The Gorilla

The Hoolock, or White-Browed Gibbon

The Tasmanian Devil

The South American Eyra

The Ethiopian Aardvark

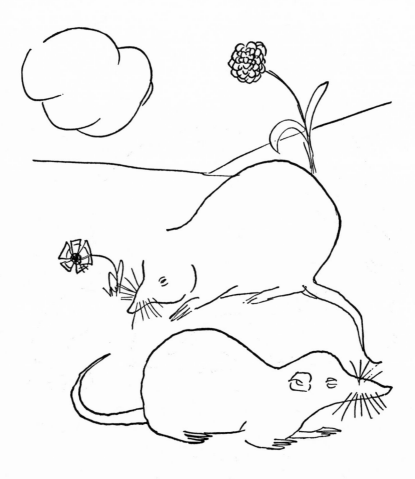

The Spider Muck-Shrew and Common Shrew

The Rock-Jumping Shrew

Bosman's Potto

The Duck-Billed Platypus

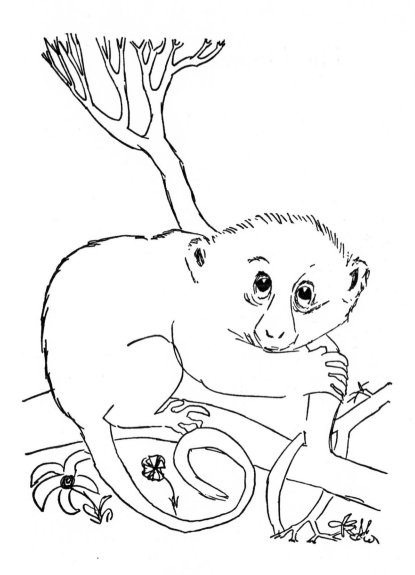

The Gentile Lemur

The Hound and the Gun

1

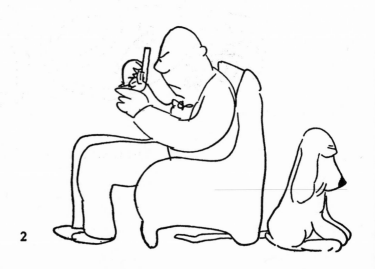

2

3

4

5

Europe

Left Bank Hotel

Paris Street

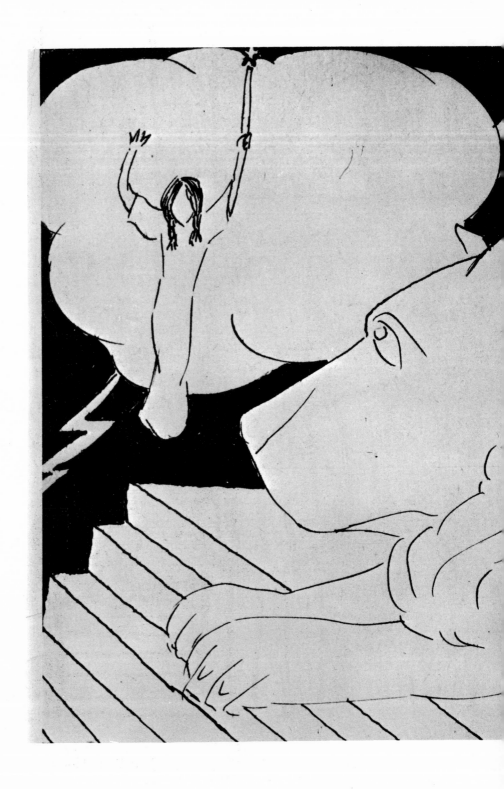

Hope After Hannibal:

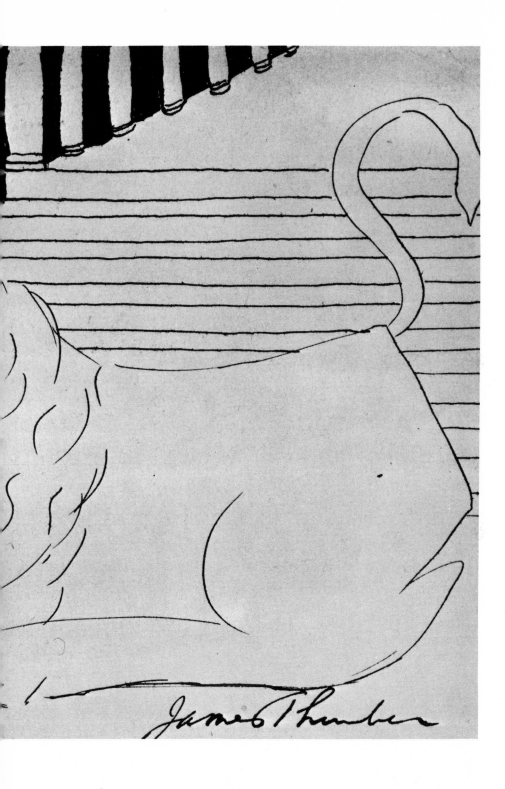

Rome, 1937

Nature Vivant aux Pommes

Mainly Men and Women

2

"If you can keep a secret, I'll tell you how my husband died."

"I assume, then, that you regard yourself as omniscient.
If I am wrong, correct me!"

"Your husband has talked about nothing but you, Mrs. Miller."

"You're going a bit far, Miss Blanchard."

"There go the most
intelligent of all
animals."

"You gah dam pussy cats!"

Youth

Fourth of July

"Let me take your hat, Mr. Williams."

"Shut up, Prince! What's biting you?"

"Now I'm going to go in over your horns!"

"What the hell ever happened to the old-fashioned love story?"

"You tell me if I bend my knees, Sugar."

"He's given up everything for a whole year."

"He got aphasia and forgot where I lived."

"Well, don't come and look at the rainbow then, you big ape!"

"The trouble with me is I can never say no."

"Here's to the old-time saloon, stranger!"

"Laissez faire and let laissez faire is what I believe in."

"No, I won't apologize—and neither will your father."

"She built up her personality, but she's undermined her character."

"Will you be good enough to dance this outside?"

Shakespeare

Hamlet and Ophelia

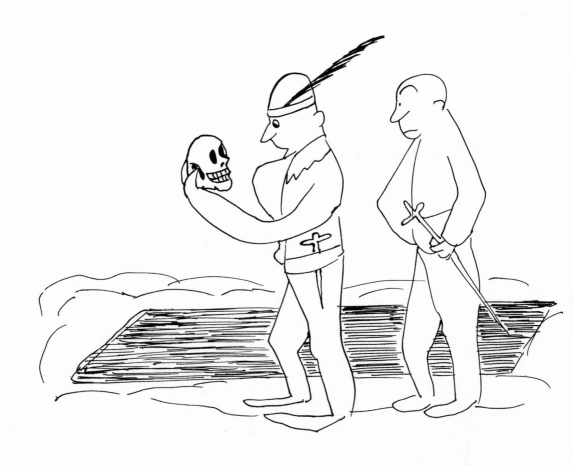

"Alas, poor Yorick!"

Ophelia

Cordelia, Lear and Gloucester

Othello and Desdemona

Lady Macbeth

Romeo and Juliet

Death of Cleopatra

The Hound
and the Hare

Self-
Portraits
and Portraits

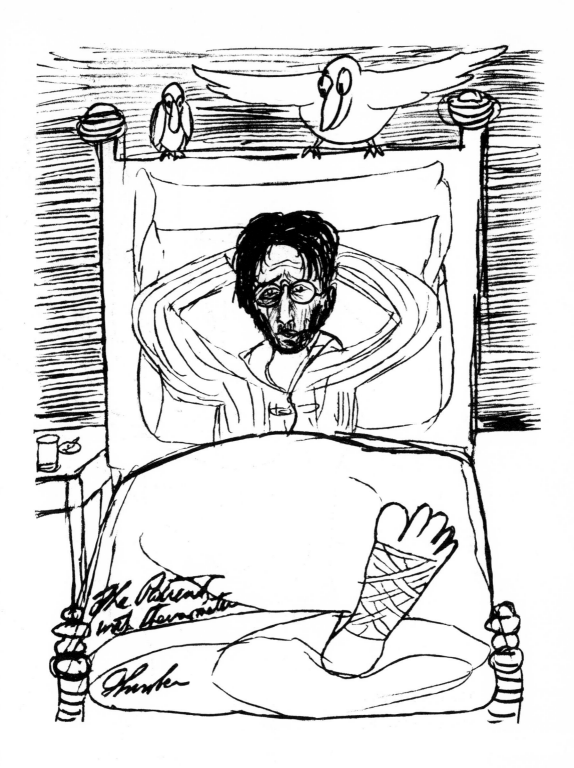

The Patient with Bursomitis

Thurber

The Reading Hour:

Thurber and Sandburg

After-Dinner Music:

Thurber and Sandburg

Winston Churchill

Famous Poems

Illustrated

The Raven
by Edgar Allan Poe

Once upon a midnight dreary, while I pondered, weak and weary,
Over many a quaint and curious volume of forgotten lore,—
While I nodded, nearly napping, suddenly there came a tapping,
As of someone gently rapping, rapping at my chamber door.
" 'Tis some visitor," I muttered, "tapping at my chamber door;
      Only this, and nothing more."

Presently my soul grew stronger; hesitating then no longer,
"Sir," said I, "or madam, truly your forgiveness I implore;
But the fact is, I was napping, and so gently you came rapping,
And so faintly you came tapping, tapping at my chamber door,
That I scarce was sure I heard you."—Here I opened wide the door;
　　　　Darkness there, and nothing more.

Open then I flung the shutter, when, with many a flirt and flutter,
In there stepped a stately raven of the saintly days of yore.
Not the least obeisance made he; not an instant stopped or stayed he;
But, with mien of lord or lady, perched above my chamber door,—
Perched above a bust of Pallas, just above my chamber door,—
      Perched, and sat, and nothing more.

"Prophet!" said I, "thing of evil!—prophet still, if bird or devil!
By that heaven that bends above us,—by that God we both adore,
Tell this soul with sorrow laden, if, within the distant Aidenn,
It shall clasp a sainted maiden, whom the angels name Lenore,
Clasp a fair and radiant maiden, whom the angels name Lenore!"
        Quoth the raven, "Nevermore!"

"Be that word our sign of parting, bird or fiend!" I shrieked, upstarting,—
"Get thee back into the tempest and the night's Plutonian shore!
Leave no black plume as a token of that lie thy should hath spoken!
Leave my loneliness unbroken!—quit the bust above my door!
Take thy beak from out my heart, and take thy form from off my door!"
        Quoth the raven, "Nevermore!"

And the raven, never flitting, still is sitting, still is sitting
On the pallid bust of Pallas just above my chamber door;
And his eyes have all the seeming of a demon that is dreaming,
And the lamplight o'er him streaming throws his shadow on the floor;
And my soul from out that shadow that lies floating on the floor
        Shall be lifted—*nevermore!*

Locksley Hall
by Alfred, Lord Tennyson

Comrades, leave me here a little, while as yet 'tis early morn;
Leave me here, and when you want me, sound upon the bugle horn.

'Tis the place, and all around it, as of old, the curlews call,
Dreary gleams about the moorland, flying over Locksley Hall.

In the spring a livelier iris changes on the burnished dove;
In the spring a young man's fancy lightly turns to thoughts of love.

O my cousin, shallow-hearted! O, my Amy, mine no more!
O the dreary, dreary moorland! O the barren, barren shore!

Is it well to wish thee happy?—having known me; to decline
On a range of lower feelings and a narrower heart than mine!

As the husband is, the wife is; thou art mated with a clown,
And the grossness of his nature will have weight to drag thee down.

Like a dog, he hunts in dreams; and thou are staring at the wall,
Where the dying night-lamp flickers, and the shadows rise and fall.

Then a hand shall pass before thee, pointing to his drunken sleep,
To thy widowed marriage-pillows, to the tears that thou wilt weep.

Hark! my merry comrades call me, sounding on the bugle-horn,—
They to whom my foolish passion were a target for their scorn.
. . . I will take some savage woman, she shall rear my dusky race.

Iron-jointed, supple-sinewed, they shall dive, and they shall run,
Catch the wild goat by the hair, and hurl their lances in the sun.

Fool, again the dream, the fancy! but I *know* my words are wild . . .

O, I see the crescent promise of my spirit hath not set;
Ancient founts of inspiration well through all my fancy yet.

. . . a long farewell to Locksley Hall!
Now for me the woods may wither, now for me the roof-tree fall.

Comes a vapor from the margin, blackening over heath and holt,
Cramming all the blast before it, in its breast a thunderbolt.

Let it fall on Locksley Hall, with rain or hail, or fire or snow;
For the mighty wind arises, roaring seaward, and I go.

The Glove and the Lions
by Leigh Hunt

King Francis was a hearty king, and loved a royal sport,
And one day, as his lions fought, sat looking at the court.
The nobles filled the benches, and the ladies in their pride,
And 'mongst them sat the Count de Lorge, with one for whom he sighed:
And truly 'twas a gallant thing to see that crowning show,
Valor and love, and a king above, and the royal beasts below.

Ramped and roared the lions, with horrid laughing jaws;
They bit, they glared, gave blows like beams, a wind went with their paws;
With wallowing might and stifled roar they rolled on one another,
Till all the pit with sand and mane was in a thunderous smother.

The bloody foam above the bars came whisking through the air;
Said Francis then, "Faith, gentlemen, we're better here than there."
De Lorge's love o'erheard the King, a beauteous lively dame,
With smiling lips and sharp bright eyes, which always seemed the same;
She thought, "The Count, my lover, is brave as brave can be;
He surely would do wondrous things to show his love of me;
King, ladies, lovers, all look on; the occasion is divine;
I'll drop my glove, to prove his love; great glory will be mine."
She dropped her glove, to prove his love, then looked at him and smiled;

He bowed, and in a moment leaped among the lions wild;

The leap was quick, return was quick, he has regained his place,
Then threw the glove, but not with love, right in the lady's face.
"By Heaven," said Francis, "rightly done!" and he rose from where he sat;
"No love," quoth he, "but vanity, sets love a task like that."

Ben Bolt

by Thomas Dunn English

Don't you remember sweet Alice, Ben Bolt—
Sweet Alice whose hair was so brown,
Who wept with delight when you gave her a smile,
And trembled with fear at your frown?

In the old churchyard in the valley, Ben Bolt,
    In a corner abscure and alone,
They have fitted a slab of the granite so gray
    And Alice lies under the stone.

And don't you remember the school, Ben Bolt,
    With the master so cruel and grim,
And the shaded nook in the running brook
    Where the children went to swim?

Grass grows on the master's grave, Ben Bolt,
    The spring of the brook is dry,
And of all the boys who were schoolmates then
    There are only you and I.

Lochinvar
by Sir Walter Scott

O, young Lochinvar is come out of the west,
Through all the wide Border his steed was the best;
And, save his good broadsword, he weapon had none,
He rode all unarmed, and he rode all alone.
So faithful in love, and so dauntless in war,
There never was knight like the young Lochinvar.

But, ere he alighted at Netherby gate,
The bride had consented, the gallant came late;
For a laggard in love, and a dastard in war,
Was to wed the fair Ellen of brave Lochinvar.

So boldly he entered the Netherby Hall,
Among bridesmen, and kinsmen, and brothers, and all.
Then spoke the bride's father, his hand on his sword
(For the poor craven bridegroom said never a word),

"O come ye in peace here, or come ye in war,
Or to dance at our bridal, young Lord Lochinvar?"

"I long wooed your daughter, my suit you denied—
Love swells like the Solway, but ebbs like its tide—
And now I am come, with this lost love of mine,
To lead but one measure, drink one cup of wine.
There are maidens in Scotland more lovely by far,
That would gladly be bride to the young Lochinvar."

The bride kissed the goblet; the knight took it up,
He quaffed off the wine, and threw down the cup.
She looked down to blush, and she looked up to sigh,
With a smile on her lips, and a tear in her eye.
He took her soft hand, ere her mother could bar—
"Now tread we a measure," said young Lochinvar.

So stately his form, and so lovely her face,
That never a hall such a galliard did grace;

While her mother did fret, and her father did fume,
And the bridegroom stood dangling his bonnet and plume . . .

One touch to her hand, and one word in her ear,
When they reached the hall door, and the charger stood near;
So light to the croupe the fair lady he swung,
So light to the saddle before her he sprung;
"She is won! we are gone! Over bank, bush, and scaur;
They'll have fleet steeds that follow," quoth young Lochinvar.

There was mounting 'mong Graemes of the Netherby clan;
Forsters, Fenwicks, and Musgraves, they rode and they ran;
There was racing and chasing on Cannobie Lee,
But the lost bride of Netherby ne'er did they see.
So daring in love, and so dauntless in war,
Have ye e'er heard of gallant like young Lochinvar?

The Hound and the Hat

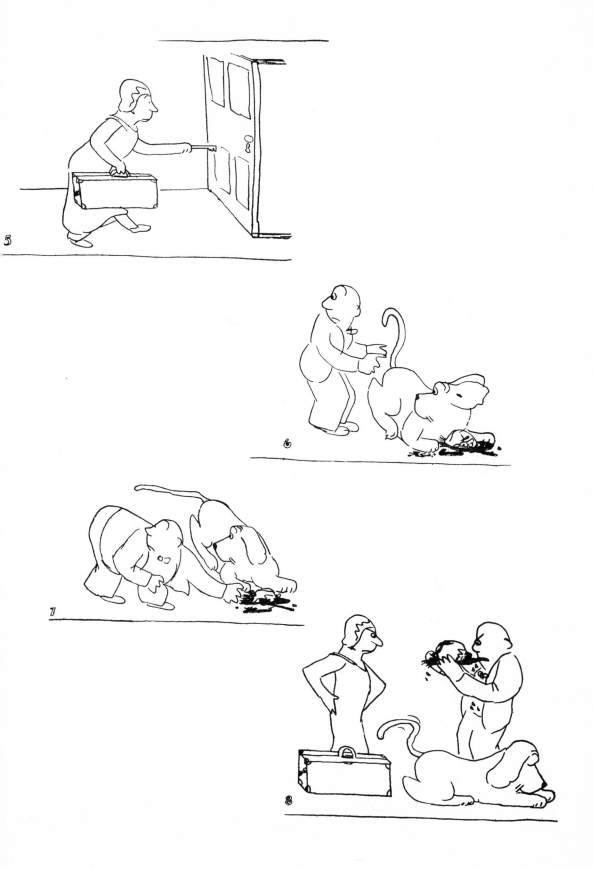

Mainly Men and Women
3

"Hello, dear! How's everything in the Marts of Trade?"

"Are you two looking for trouble, Mister?"

"I wouldn't rent this room
to everybody, Mr. Spencer.
This is where my husband
lost his mind."

"Which you am I talking to now?"

Algonquin Lobby

Waiter

"I wouldn't even let Cary Grant lounge around my house
in the afternoon."

"George! If that's you I'll never forgive you!"

"He hates people."

"Have you no code, man?"

"Comb the woods!"

American Folk Dance

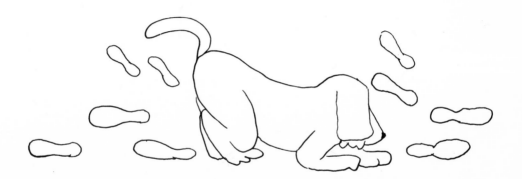

Destinations

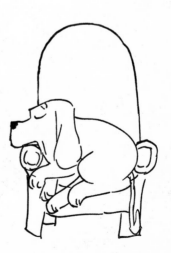

Christmas Cards

Parties

Some People Dropped In for Cocktails

Cocktail Party, 1937

"When I wore a tulip..."

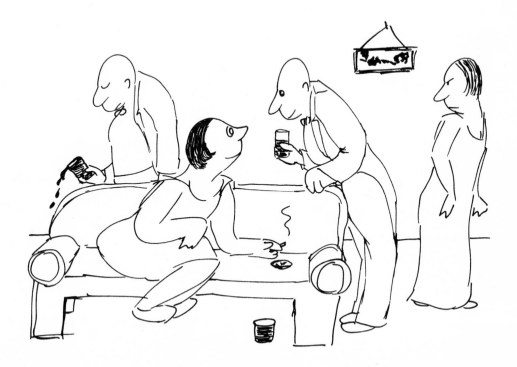

Love

First Husband Down

The Bawling Out

"The party's breaking up, darling."

Berserk

The Brawl

The Fog

Four O'Clock in the Morning

Word Dances

The first drawing in this section decorated the curtain that rose on the first act of *A Thurber Carnival,* a Broadway revue back in 1960. The last drawing was, fittingly enough, the final curtain. In between, the drawings with their captions represent lines from the opening and closing numbers of the revue, both called "word dances." A few liberties have been taken in fitting stage dialogue to pictures, but not nearly as many as the author himself took in fitting his own picture captions to stage dialogue. It all evens up in the end.

"You may call it sleepwalking, but I say she's promiscuous."

"My wife wants to spend Halloween with her first husband."

"Well, if I called the wrong number, why did you
answer the phone?"

"I know he's terribly nervous, but I'm sure he meant it as a pass at me."

"My husband went up to bed one night and was never seen again."

"She never saw much of her husband until <u>after</u> they were separated."

"She says he proposed something on their wedding night her own brother wouldn't have suggested."

"Walter Lippmann scares me this morning."

"I told the analyst everything except my experience with Mr. Rinesfoos."

"I want you to meet Miss Gorce. Miss Gorce is in the embalming game."

"Where did you get
those big brown eyes
and that tiny mind?"

"She's all I know about
Bryn Mawr, and
all I need to know."

"You wait here and I'll bring the etchings down."

"He knows all about art,
but he doesn't know
what he likes."

"So I said to the bank teller,
'How can I be overdrawn
when I have all these checks
left?'"

"He's having all his books translated into French.
They lose something in the original."

"Why don't you get dressed then, and go to pieces like a man?"

"My husband wanted to live in sin, even <u>after</u> we were married."

Let us ponder this basic fact about the human: Ahead
of every man, not behind him, is a woman.

Final Curtain

Index

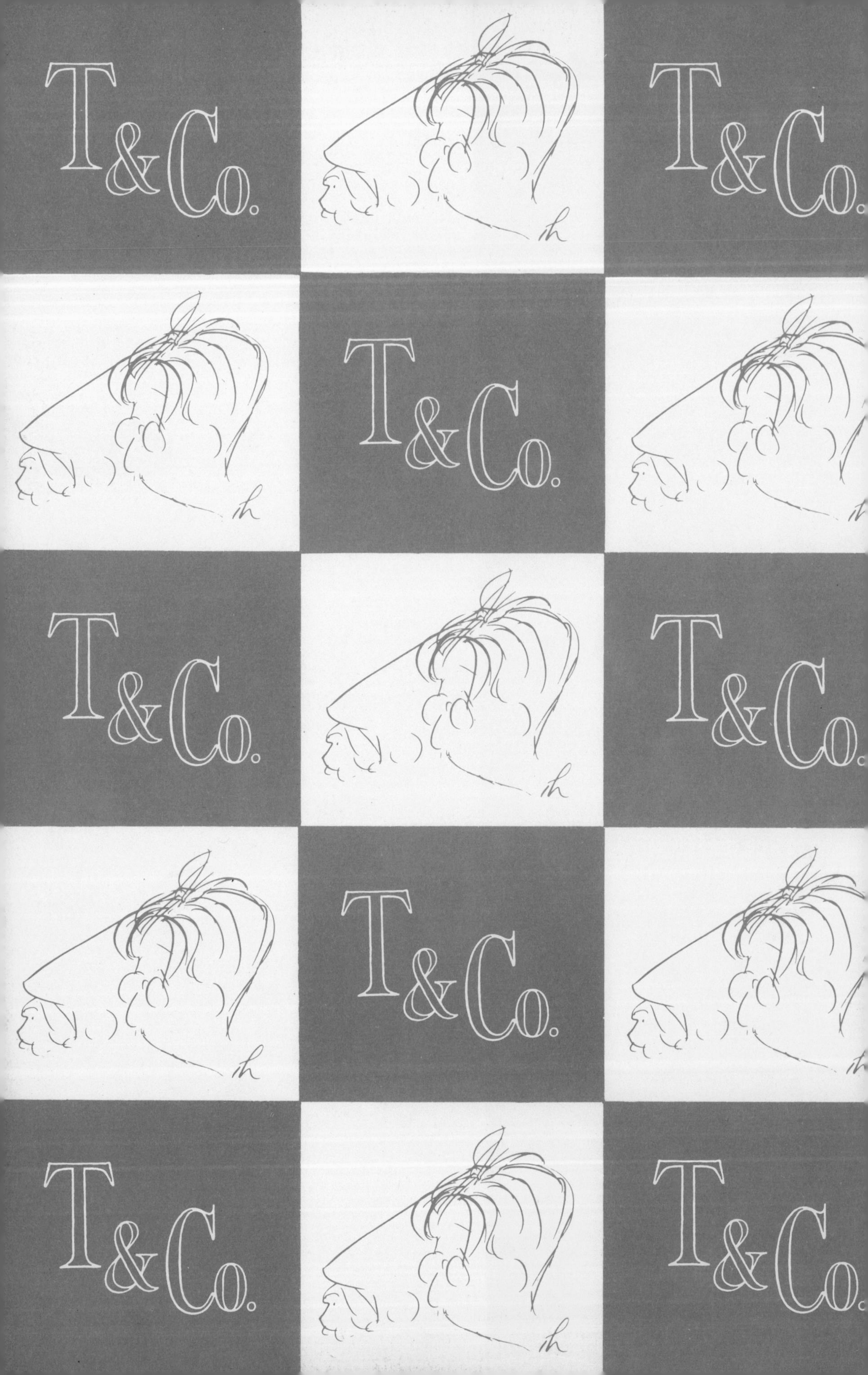
T&Co.